MW01285011

This Book Belongs To:

____

Made in the USA
Middletown, DE
27 October 2023

41469555R00057